D1235276

Basic Mathematics Skillbuilder for Middle Schoolers

Ted A. Akinyanju

ISBN Number 1-57087-419-0

Professional Press
Chapel Hill, NC 27515-4371

Manufactured in the United States of America
99 00 01 02 03   10 9 8 7 6 5 4 3 2 1

PREFACE

This book is intended as a convenient reference for the Middle or freshman High School student during the regular school year and to provide practice and tutoring during the summer months. Its purpose is to help strengthen mathematical skills. Essential topics of basic mathematics are covered and easy-to-understand steps are used in examples. There is practice in Geometry, Fractions, Decimal Fractions, Algebra and Graphing.

It may not be possible to remember all skills learned during the school year after the summer fun. And since learning is a continuous process, it would be a good idea to use a little time to get ready. Skills learned in previous periods should serve as prerequisites for skills to be learned in subsequent periods.

TO THE PARENT

The needs of the marginally prepared student can be, and often are, overlooked. Encouraging your Middle/High School student to use part (a few weeks) of the summer break to prepare for the new school year can be very rewarding. Such an endeavor will help develop/reinforce skills and also build confidence.

Your involvement will help your child to step ahead.

CONTENTS

CHAPTER 1—WEIGHTS AND MEASURES 1

METRIC (LINEAR LENGTH) 1
CUSTOMARY (LINEAR LENGTH) 1
METRIC (CAPACITY OR VOLUME) 1
LIQUID MEASURE (CUSTOMARY-CAPACITY) 2
METRIC (WEIGHT-MASS) 2
CUSTOMARY (WEIGHT) 2
CONVERSIONS BETWEEN METRIC AND
    CUSTOMARY UNITS 3
LENGTH 3
AREA 3
VOLUME 3
CAPACITY OR VOLUME (LIQUID) 3
MASS 4
EXERCISES 1-1 (Weights and Measures) 5
FORMULAS
    AREAS 6
    VOLUMES 9
    PERIMETERS 11
    EXERCISES 1-2 Formulas 13

CHAPTER 2—GEOMETRIC IDEAS 19

TYPES OF ANGLES 22
EXERCISES 2-1 31

CHAPTER 3—FRACTIONS 33

EXERCISES 3-1 36
ADDITION AND SUBTRACTION OF FRACTIONS 37
EXERCISES 3-2 40
EXERCISES 3-3 42
MULTIPLICATION AND DIVISION OF FRACTIONS .. 42
EXERCISES 3-4 44
THE RECIPROCAL 44
DIVISION BY A FRACTION 45

CHAPTER 4—MULTIPLYING DECIMAL FRACTIONS 47

MULTIPLYING DECIMAL FRACTIONS
BY POWERS OF TEN 48
EXERCISES 4-1 49
DIVIDING DECIMAL FRACTIONS 49
DIVIDING DECIMAL FRACTIONS BY
POWERS OF TEN 50
EXERCISES 4-2 51
EVALUATING NUMERICAL EXPRESSIONS
(Order of Operations) 51

CHAPTER 5—INTRODUCTION TO ALGEBRA 53

SYMBOLS/OPERATIONAL SIGNS 54
EQUATIONS 54
EXERCISES 5-1 57

CHAPTER 6—INEQUALITIES 59

THE NUMBER LINE 60
EXERCISES 6-1 65

CHAPTER 7—GRAPHING LINEAR EQUATIONS 67

THE NUMBER LINE 67
THE RECTANGULAR COORDINATE SYSTEM 67
THE COORDINATE PLANE 68
EXERCISES 7-1 70
GRAPHS OF LINEAR EQUATIONS 71
EXERCISES 7-2 74
THE INTERCEPTS OF A LINE 74
EXERCISES 7-3 76
THE SLOPE OF A LINE 76
EXERCISES 7-4 80

ANSWERS TO PROBLEMS 81

INDEX 87

CHAPTER 1
WEIGHTS AND MEASURES

METRIC (LINEAR LENGTH)

10 millimeters (mm) = 1 centimeter (cm)
10 centimeters (cm) = 1 decimeter (dm)
10 decimeters (dm) = 1 meter (m)
10 meters (m) = 1 decameter (dam)
10 decameters (dam) = 1 hectometer (hm)
10 hectometers (hm) = 1 kilometer (km)
*1 kilo = 1000

CUSTOMARY (LINEAR LENGTH)

12 inches (in) = 1 foot (ft)
3 feet (ft) = 1 yard (yd)
5280 feet (ft) = 1 mile (mi)
1760 yards (yd) = 1 mile

METRIC (CAPACITY OR VOLUME)

10 milliliters (ml) = 1 centiliter (cl)
10 centiliters (cl) = 1 deciliter (dl)
10 deciliters (dl) = 1 liter (1)
10 liters (l) = 1 decaliter (dal)
10 decaliters (dal) = 1 hectoliter (hl)
10 hectoliters (hl) = 1 kiloliter (kl)

LIQUID MEASURE (CUSTOMARY—CAPACITY)

4 fluid ounces (fl. oz)	=	1 gill (gl)
4 gills (gl)	=	1 pint (pt)
2 pints (pt)	=	1 quart (qt)
4 quarts (qt)	=	1 gallon

METRIC (WEIGHT-MASS)   ***gram is unit of mass**

1000 milligrams	=	1 gram
1000 grams	=	1 kilogram
1000 kilograms	=	1 metric ton
		(megagram)
		*1 mega = 1,000,000

CUSTOMARY (WEIGHT)

16 drams	=	1 ounce (oz)
16 ounces (oz)	=	1 pound (lb)
100 pounds (lb)	=	1 hundredweight
		(cwt)
2000 pounds	=	1 ton

CONVERSIONS BETWEEN METRIC AND CUSTOMARY UNITS

LENGTH:

1 millimeter = 0.04 inch
(1 inch = 25.4 millimeters)
1 meter = 3.3 feet
1 kilometer = 0.6 mile

AREA:

1 square centimeter = 0.16 square inch
1 square meter = 11 square feet
1 square meter = 1.2 square yards

VOLUME:

1 cubic centimeter = 0.06 cubic inch
1 cubic meter = 35 cubic feet

CAPACITY OR VOLUME (LIQUID):

1 liter = 1.057 quarts
1 cubic meter = 250 gallons

MASS:

$$1 \text{ gram} = 0.035 \text{ ounce}$$
$$1 \text{ kilogram} = 2.2 \text{ pounds}$$

Examples:

1. **Convert 100 meters to yards.**

   From tables: 1 meter = 3.3 feet
   3 feet = 1 yard

   Therefore 100 m = 3.3 ft. (100) = 330 ft.
   and 1 ft. = $\frac{1}{3}$ yd.

   330 ft. = $\frac{1}{3}$ yd. (330) = $\frac{330}{3}$ yd. = 110 yd.

2. **Convert 10 liters to gallons**

   From tables: 1 liter = 1.057 quarts
   4 quarts = 1 gallon

   Therefore 10 liters = 1.057 quarts (10) =
   10.57 quarts and 1 quart = $\frac{1}{4}$ gallon

   10.57 quarts = $\frac{1}{4}$ gallon (10.57) =
   $\frac{10.57}{4}$ gallons = 2.64 gallons

4

EXERCISES 1-1 (Weights and Measures)

Using the tables, complete the following:

1.   1 km = _____ mm
2.   7 mm = _____ cm
3.   1000 mm = _____ m
4.   675 ml = _____ l
5.   86 cl = _____ l
6.   5000 ml = _____ l
7.   1 kg = _____ mg
8.   1.4 kg = _____ g
9.   0.5 kg = _____ g
10. 1000 m = _____ km
11. 0.625 lb. = _____ oz.
12. 5 gal. = _____ qt.
13. 3 mi. = _____ ft.
14. 1 gal. 1 qt. = _____ pt.

Perform the following conversions:

15. 400 m = _____ yd.
16. 4 mi. = _____ km
17. 3.2 in. = _____ mm
18. 3.4 sq. yd. = _____ sq. ft.
19. 1 l = _____ gal.
20. 1 lb. = _____ kg.

FORMULAS

AREAS: Area is the measure of region in a simple closed curve

RECTANGLE:

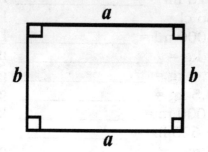

Area = $a.b$
where a = length of base
b = width

TRIANGLE:

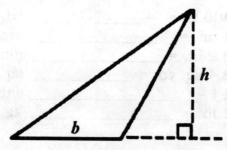

Area = $\frac{1}{2}.b.h$
where b = length of base
h = height

PARALLELOGRAM:

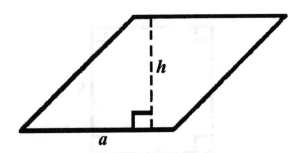

Area = $a.h$
where a = length of the base
h = height

CIRCLE:

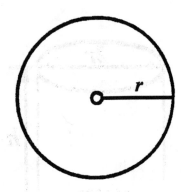

Area = $\pi\, r^2$
where r = radius
= diameter/2
pi (π) = 3.14

SQUARE:

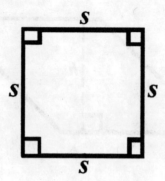

Area = s.s
where s = length of side

CYLINDER:

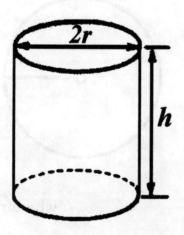

Area (lateral) = 2 π rh
Area (total) = 2 π r (r + h)

VOLUMES: Volume is the measure of space
enclosed by a solid figure.

PRISM:

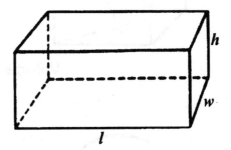

Volume = $l.w.h$

CONE:

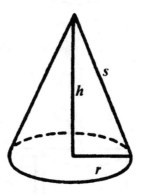

Volume= $\frac{1}{3} \pi r^2 h$
where r = radius of base

TRIANGULAR PRISM:

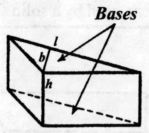

Bases

Volume = $\frac{1}{2}.b.l.h$

SPHERE:

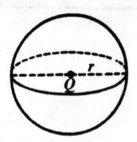

Volume = $\frac{4}{3}\pi r^3$

CYLINDER:

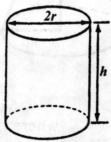

Volume = $\pi r^2 h$
where r = radius of base

PERIMETERS:

Perimeter of a figure is the total distance around the figure.

POLYGON: Perimeter is sum of the lengths of its sides.

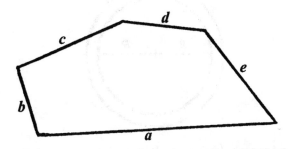

Perimeter = $a+b+c+d+e$

RECTANGLE:

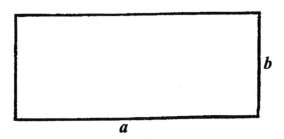

Perimeter = $2.a + 2.b = 2(a + b)$

CIRCLE: The distance around a circle is
called its CIRCUMFERENCE).

- Diameter is twice the Radius. This means
Radius = Diameter/2

- Diameter divides the circle in halves.

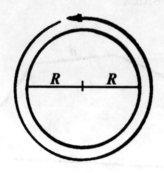

Circumference = pi multiplied by diameter = πD

or

Circumference = $2 \pi R$

EXERCISES 1-2 Formulas

Find the perimeter of each of the following figures.

1.

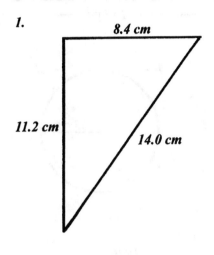

2.

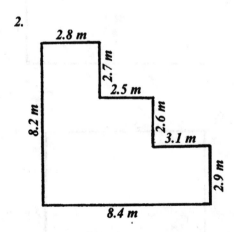

3.

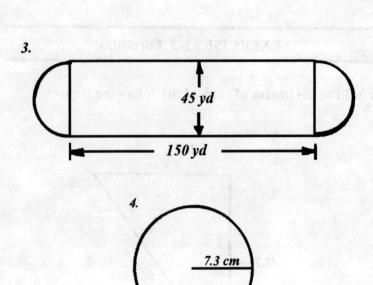

45 yd

150 yd

4.

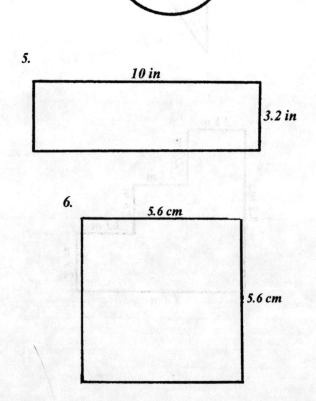

7.3 cm

5.

10 in

3.2 in

6.

5.6 cm

5.6 cm

14

Find the area of each region shown.

7.

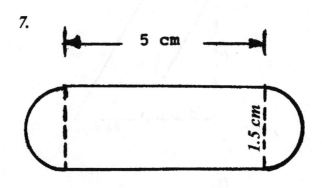

8.

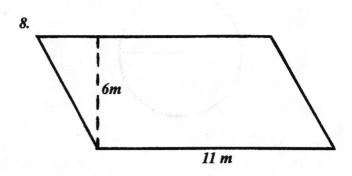

9.

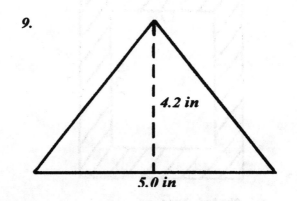

10.

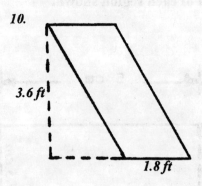

3.6 ft

1.8 ft

11.

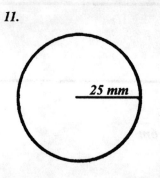

25 mm

12.

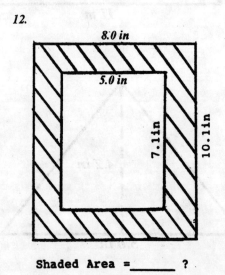

8.0 in

5.0 in

7.1 in

10.1 in

Shaded Area = _____ ?

16

Find the volume of each figure shown:

13.

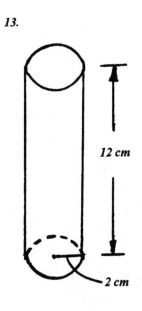

12 cm

2 cm

14.

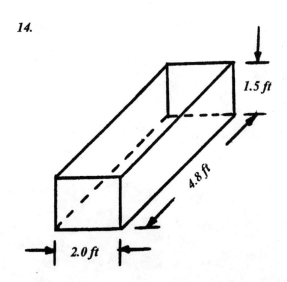

1.5 ft

4.8 ft

2.0 ft

CHAPTER 2
GEOMETRIC IDEAS

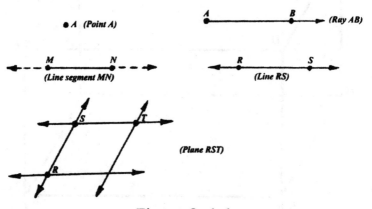

Figure 2. 1-1

* A LINE contains at least two points.
* A RAY is half-line with an endpoint
* A LINE SEGMENT is the portion of a line
  between the points and including the points as
  end points.
* A PLANE can be determined by three points
  not on the same line.
* Two lines are PARALLEL if they lie in the same
  plane and will never intersect.
* POINT OF INTERSECTION is the point at
  which two or more lines intersect.
* SKEW LINES are two lines in different planes
  that do not intersect.

Example:

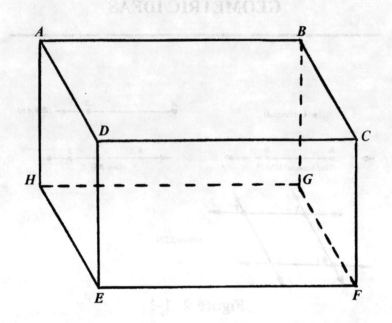

Figure 2. 1-2

$\overleftrightarrow{AB}$ and $\overleftrightarrow{CD}$ are parallel ($\overleftrightarrow{AB}$ // $\overleftrightarrow{CD}$)

$\overleftrightarrow{EF}$ and $\overleftrightarrow{DC}$ are parallel ($\overleftrightarrow{EF}$ // $\overleftrightarrow{DC}$)

$\overleftrightarrow{AH}$ and $\overleftrightarrow{EF}$ are SKEW LINES

$\overleftrightarrow{CD}$ and $\overleftrightarrow{HG}$ are SKEW LINES

Can you find other PARALLEL and SKEW lines?

An angle is the union of two rays that have a common end-point. The common end-point is called the VERTEX of the angle and the two rays are called the SIDES of the angle.

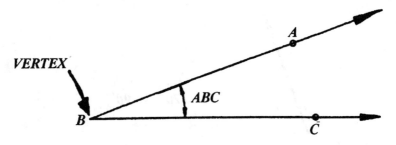

*A RIGHT ANGLE is represented by the symbol ⌐

If two lines intersect so that right angles are formed, the lines are said to be PERPENDICULAR.

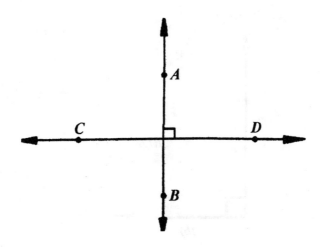

*The symbol ⊥ represents prependicularity.

The unit of measure for an angle is the DEGREE. The symbol ° represents degree.

Types of Angles:

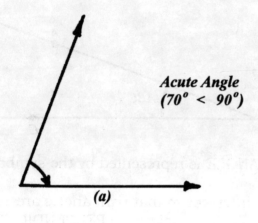

Acute Angle
(70° < 90°)

(a)

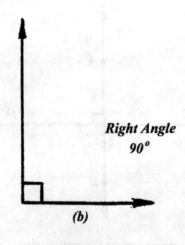

Right Angle
90°

(b)

FIGURE 2. 1-2

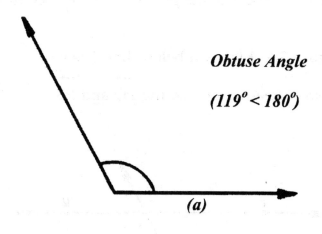

Obtuse Angle

(119° < 180°)

(a)

Straight Angle

180°

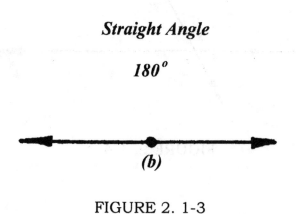

(b)

FIGURE 2. 1-3

*In the discussion of angles, the measure of an angle will be written as m∠.

A TRANSVERSAL is a line that intersects two or more lines in the same plane at different points.

In figure 2.1-4 (shown below) line 1 is a TRANSVERSAL, intersecting $\overleftrightarrow{PQ}$ and $\overleftrightarrow{RS}$

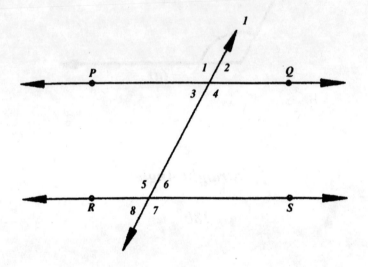

FIGURE 2. 1-4

CORRESPONDING ANGLES are angles located at the same position with respect to the transversal and the intersected lines. In figure 2.1-4 (above),

$$\angle 1 \text{ and } \angle 5 \qquad \angle 2 \text{ and } \angle 6$$
$$\angle 3 \text{ and } \angle 8 \qquad \angle 4 \text{ and } \angle 7$$

are pairs of corresponding angles.

*The angles in a pair of corresponding angles are equal in measure.

ALTERNATE INTERIOR ANGLES are angles interior to the intersected lines but on alternate sides of the transversal. In figure 2.1-4 (above),

$$\angle 3 \text{ and } \angle 6 \qquad \angle 4 \text{ and } \angle 5$$

are pairs of alternate interior angles.

*The angles in a pair of alternate interior angles are equal in measure.

COMPLEMENTARY ANGLES: Two angles are complementary when the sum of their measures is 90°.

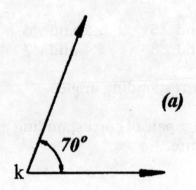

(a)

m∠k + m∠l = 70° + 20° = 90°

∠k and ∠l are complementary.

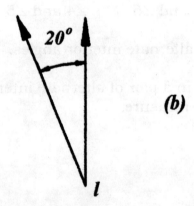

(b)

FIGURE 2. 1-5

SUPPLEMENTARY ANGLES: Two angles are supplementary when the sum of their measures is 180°.

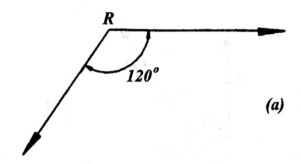

(a)

m∠R + m∠S = 120° + 60° = 180°

∠R and ∠S are supplementary

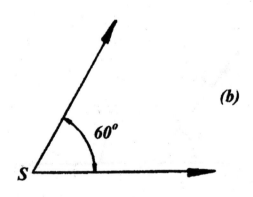

(b)

FIGURE 2. 1-6

ADJACENT ANGLES: Two angles that share a common side, but do not overlap each other are called Adjacent Angles.

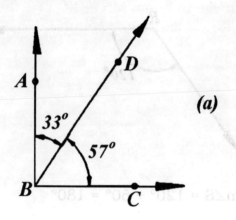

(a)

∠ABD and ∠DBC are adjacent

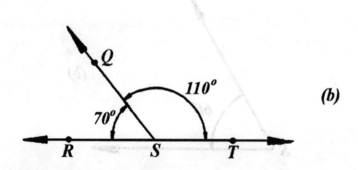

(b)

m∠RSQ + m∠TSQ = 180°
(adjacent angles on a straight line)

FIGURE 2. 1-7

Example 1:

In the figure shown below, $\overleftrightarrow{MN}$ // $\overleftrightarrow{OP}$. Find the measure of (a) ∠6, (b) ∠7 and (c) ∠8

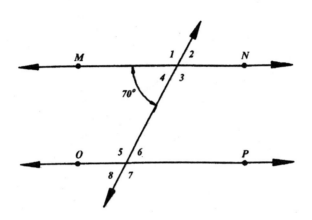

Solution:

(a) ∠4 = ∠6 (alternate interior angles)
Since ∠4 = 70°, therefore ∠4 = ∠6 = 70°.

(b) ∠6 and ∠7 are supplementary angles with measure of 180°.

We now know that ∠6 = 70°.
∠7 = 180° - ∠6 = 180° - 70° = 110°.

(c) ∠4 and ∠8 are corresponding angles.
Since ∠4 has a measure of 70°,
therefore ∠4 = ∠8 = 70°.

Note that ∠7 and ∠8 are also supplementary angles.

29

VERTICAL ANGLES: When two lines intersect, the angles that are not adjacent to each other are called *vertical angles.* Vertical Angles are always equal in measure.

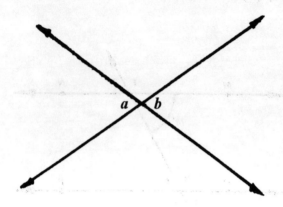

FIGURE 2. 1-8

Find the measure of a complement of an angle of the given measure.

1. 15°   2. 79°   3. 50°   4. 47°

Find the measure of a supplement of an angle of the given measure.

5. 71°   6. 135°   7. 85°   8. 55°

9. **Give the measure of each of the angles shown below.**

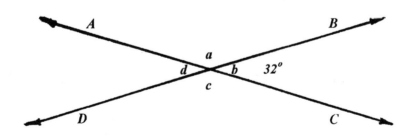

FIGURE 2. 1-9

CHAPTER 3
FRACTIONS

A **FRACTION** may contain any number or symbol representing a number in its numerator or denominator. It can therefore be rational, irrational or imaginary. (In this text, we will consider rational numbers only).

Every rational number may be written in the form $\frac{a}{b}$ where a and b are integers. The expression $\frac{a}{b}$ is called a fraction.

The numbers $\frac{3}{5}$ and $\frac{-7}{4}$ are fractions, and they are also rational.

*Every rational number $\frac{a}{b}$ also has a decimal equivalent which can be determined by dividing a by b.

$$\frac{2}{50} = 0.04 \quad \text{and} \quad \frac{3}{2} = 1.5$$

RULE: To change a **MIXED NUMBER** to a fraction (improper fraction). Multiply the whole number by the denominator, add the numerator and place this sum over the denominator.

Examples:

$$6\frac{3}{5} = \frac{(6 \times 5) + 3}{5} = \frac{33}{5} \quad \text{and} \quad 2\frac{1}{3} = \frac{(2 \times 3) + 1}{3} = \frac{7}{3}$$

A **SIMPLE FRACTION** is one in which the numerator and denominator are whole numbers.

Examples: $\frac{1}{2}$, $\frac{3}{4}$, $\frac{7}{2}$, $\frac{9}{5}$

A **COMPLEX FRACTION** is one in which the numerator and/or the denominator are both fractions.

Examples: $\dfrac{\frac{3}{4}}{\frac{1}{5}}$, $\dfrac{\frac{2}{5}}{6}$, $\dfrac{6\frac{1}{2}}{4}$, $\dfrac{7}{\frac{8}{9}}$

A **PROPER FRACTION** is one in which the numerator is smaller than the denominator.

Examples: $\frac{1}{4}$, $\frac{2}{3}$, $\frac{7}{9}$, $\frac{30}{37}$

AN **IMPROPER FRACTION** is one in which the numerator is equal to or greater than the denominator

Examples: $\frac{3}{3}$, $\frac{5}{2}$, $\frac{9}{4}$, $\frac{8}{8}$, $\frac{45}{30}$

AN **EQUIVALENT FRACTION** is one written in a different form but still has the same value as the original fraction. It can be obtained by multiplying or dividing both numerator and denominator by the same non-zero number.

Examples: $\frac{3}{4} = \frac{3}{4} \times \frac{2}{2} = \frac{6}{8}$

It can be seen that $\frac{3}{4}$ is equivalent to $\frac{6}{8}$

*To be sure you have an equivalent fraction, check the cross products.

Classify each of the following fractions as simple or complex.

1. $\dfrac{3}{7}$ 2. $\dfrac{8}{5}$ 3. $\dfrac{6}{13}$ 4. $\dfrac{\frac{2}{3}}{\frac{4}{9}}$

5. $\dfrac{2\frac{1}{4}}{4}$ 6. $\dfrac{\frac{1}{3}}{\frac{9}{4}}$ 7. $\dfrac{6}{2\frac{1}{2}}$

In exercises 8 through 13 write an equivalent fraction for each fraction by multiplying the numerator and denominator by the number in parentheses.

8. $\dfrac{5}{7}$ (3)   9. $\dfrac{21}{25}$ (2)   10. $\dfrac{7}{3}$ (4)

11. $\dfrac{5}{15}$ (5)   12. $\dfrac{11}{33}$ (3)   13. $\dfrac{2}{5}$ (6)

In exercises 14 through 20 divide the numerator and denominator of each fraction by the number in parentheses to write an equivalent fraction.

14. $\dfrac{16}{12}$ (4)　　15. $\dfrac{60}{93}$ (3)　　16. $\dfrac{44}{77}$ (11)

17. $\dfrac{45}{81}$ (9)　　18. $\dfrac{15}{75}$ (15)　　19. $\dfrac{120}{243}$ (3)

20. $\dfrac{72}{56}$ (8)

In exercises 21 through 24 determine whether or not the pairs of fractions are equivalent.

21. $\dfrac{3}{3}$, $\dfrac{11}{11}$　　　22. $\dfrac{18}{2}$, $\dfrac{81}{9}$

23. $\dfrac{4}{8}$, $\dfrac{5}{8}$　　　24. $\dfrac{8}{3}$, $\dfrac{16}{6}$

ADDITION AND SUBTRACTION OF FRACTIONS

RULES: To add fractions having the same denominator, add their numerators and then write the resulting sum over their common denominator.

To add fractions having unlike denominators, change the fractions to equivalent fractions which have the same denominator—the least common multiple denominator (LCD).

*LCD is the number that each of the denominators will divide into with no remainder.

Example 1. $\dfrac{3}{5} + \dfrac{2}{5} = \dfrac{3+2}{5} = \dfrac{5}{5} = 1$

Example 2. $\dfrac{5}{8} + \dfrac{2}{8} = \dfrac{5+2}{8} = \dfrac{7}{8}$

Example 3. $\dfrac{3}{4} + \dfrac{2}{3}$ the LCD = 4 x 3 = 12

Solution: $\dfrac{3}{4} + \dfrac{2}{3}$

$$\dfrac{3(3) + 4(2)}{12} = \dfrac{17}{12} = 1\dfrac{5}{12}$$

Example 4. $\dfrac{5}{18} + \dfrac{7}{24}$

18 = 2 x 3 x 3
24 = 2 x 3 x 4
the LCD = 2 x 3 x 3 x 4 = 72

Solution: $\dfrac{5}{18} + \dfrac{7}{24}$

$$\dfrac{4(5) + 3(7)}{72} = \dfrac{20 + 21}{72} = \dfrac{41}{72}$$

Example 5. $1\dfrac{7}{8} + 2\dfrac{1}{3}$

Method 1: First combine the whole numbers, 1 and 2 to get 3.

Next add the fractions, $\dfrac{7}{8}$ and $\dfrac{1}{3}$ to get $\dfrac{29}{24}$ which is equal to $1\dfrac{5}{24}$.

Then combine 3 and $1\dfrac{5}{24}$ to get final answer $4\dfrac{5}{24}$.

Method 2: First change the mixed numbers to fractions; add and then simplify.

$$1\dfrac{7}{8} = \dfrac{15}{8} \quad \text{and} \quad 2\dfrac{1}{3} = \dfrac{7}{3}$$

Solution: $\dfrac{15}{8} + \dfrac{7}{3}$

LCD = 2 x 4 x 3 = 24

$$\dfrac{3(15) + 8(7)}{24} = \dfrac{45 + 56}{24} = \dfrac{101}{24} = 4\dfrac{5}{24}$$

Perform the indicated operations:

1. $\dfrac{1}{2} + \dfrac{2}{3}$ 2. $\dfrac{5}{8} + \dfrac{3}{4}$

3. $\dfrac{3}{5} + \dfrac{7}{10}$ 4. $1 + \dfrac{5}{7}$

5. $1\dfrac{1}{2} + 3\dfrac{5}{9}$ 6. $2\dfrac{1}{2} + 3\dfrac{1}{4}$

7. $\dfrac{5}{12} + 2\dfrac{7}{12}$ 8. $\dfrac{1}{3} + \dfrac{3}{4} + \dfrac{1}{2}$

RULE: To subtract fractions, find their least common denominator (LCD) and subtract the numerators.

Example 1. $\dfrac{7}{8} - \dfrac{1}{2}$ LCD = 8

Solution: $\dfrac{7}{8} - \dfrac{1}{2}$

$$\dfrac{1(7) - 4(1)}{8} = \dfrac{7 - 4}{8} = \dfrac{3}{8}$$

Example 2. $\quad 4 - 1\frac{5}{6}$

Solution: First write 4 as $\frac{4}{1}$ and $1\frac{5}{6}$ as $\frac{11}{6}$

$$\frac{4}{1} - \frac{11}{6}$$

$$LCD = 6$$

$$\frac{6(4) - 1(11)}{6} = \frac{24 - 11}{6} = \frac{13}{6} = 2\frac{1}{6}$$

Example 3. $\quad 12\frac{2}{5} - 7\frac{3}{7}$

Solution: First write $12\frac{2}{5}$ as $\frac{62}{5}$ and $7\frac{3}{7}$ as $\frac{52}{7}$

$$\frac{62}{5} - \frac{52}{7}$$

$$\frac{7(62) - 5(52)}{35} = \frac{434 - 260}{35} = \frac{174}{35} = 4\frac{34}{35}$$

Perform the indicated operations:

1. $\dfrac{3}{4} - \dfrac{1}{8}$

2. $\dfrac{5}{7} - \dfrac{3}{7}$

3. $2\dfrac{2}{3} - 1\dfrac{3}{5}$

4. $7\dfrac{1}{2} - 3\dfrac{5}{8}$

5. $9 - 1\dfrac{13}{16}$

6. $\dfrac{9}{2} - 2\dfrac{5}{6}$

MULTIPLICATION AND DIVISION OF FRACTIONS:

RULE: To multiply two fractions, find the product of the numerators divided by the product of the denominators.

$$\frac{a}{b} \times \frac{c}{d} = \frac{a \times c}{b \times d}$$

Example 1. $\dfrac{5}{6} \times \dfrac{3}{7} = \dfrac{15}{42} = \dfrac{5}{14}$

Example 2. $1\dfrac{3}{4} \times \dfrac{5}{8}$

Solution: First write $1\frac{3}{4}$ as $\frac{7}{4}$

Set Up: $\dfrac{7}{4}$ x $\dfrac{5}{8}$ = $\dfrac{7 \times 5}{4 \times 8}$ = $\dfrac{35}{32}$ = $1\frac{3}{32}$

Example 3. 6 x $7\frac{1}{8}$

Solution: First write 6 as $\frac{6}{1}$ and $7\frac{1}{8}$ as $\frac{57}{8}$.

Set Up: $\dfrac{6}{1}$ x $\dfrac{57}{8}$ = $\dfrac{6 \times 57}{1 \times 8}$ = $\dfrac{342}{8}$ = $42\frac{6}{8}$ = $42\frac{3}{4}$

Multiply

1. $\frac{4}{5}$ x 3   2. $5\frac{1}{4}$ x $2\frac{1}{3}$

3. $4\frac{7}{9}$ x $\frac{2}{5}$ 4. $1\frac{1}{4}$ x $\frac{4}{5}$

5. $\frac{15}{32}$ x $\frac{16}{25}$ 6. $\frac{11}{5}$ x $\frac{13}{33}$

7.   5 quarts of a fruit drink is prepared so that $\frac{2}{5}$ of it is orange juice, how much orange juice is used?

THE RECIPROCAL: The reciprocal of any number is 1 divided by that number. (Every number, except zero, has a reciprocal).

Example 1. The reciprocal of 3 is $\frac{1}{3}$

Example 2. The reciprocal of - 6 is -$\frac{1}{6}$

DIVISION BY A FRACTION: Dividing by a fraction requires inverting the fraction, that is using the reciprocal of the fraction.

Example 1. $\dfrac{7}{\dfrac{1}{3}} = 7 \times \dfrac{3}{1} = 21$

Example 2. $\dfrac{\dfrac{1}{2}}{\dfrac{1}{4}} = \dfrac{1}{2} \times \dfrac{4}{1} = 2$

Example 3. $\dfrac{-4}{\dfrac{-1}{2}} = -4 \times \dfrac{-2}{1} = 8$

CHAPTER 4
MULTIPLYING DECIMAL FRACTIONS

Decimal Fractions can be multiplied the same way as whole numbers except that it is required to determine the position of the decimal point in the product.

RULE: Multiply as if the decimal fractions were whole numbers. The number of decimal places in the product must equal the sum of the number of decimal places in the original decimal numbers.

Example 1.   Multiply 3.07 x .09

Solution: 3.07   (2 decimal places)
                 x .09   (2 decimal places)
                 2763
                 000
                 .2763   (4 decimal places)

Example 2.   Multiply .013 x .0022

Solution: .013   (3 decimal places)
               x .0022   (4 decimal places)
                 026
                 026
               .0000286   (7 decimal places)

Example 3.   Multiply 6.14 x 1.71

Solution: 6.14   (2 decimal places)
           x   1.71   (2 decimal places)
                614
              4298
                614
             10.4994   (4 decimal places)

MULTIPLYING DECIMAL FRACTIONS BY POWERS OF TEN

To multiply a decimal fraction by 10, 100, 1000 and so on, move the decimal point in the fraction to the right as many places as there are zeros in the multiplier.

Example. .006 x 10   = . 0   .06   = .06

          .006 x 100   = . 0   0.6   = .6

          .006 x 1000 = . 0   0   6. = 6.

Perform each of the following:

1. 11.42 x .003   2. 7.47 x 2.16

3. .6 x .5   4. .007 x .043

5. 3.2 x .009   6. 3.14 x 100

7. The volume of a box can be determined by first multiplying the length of the box by its height and then by its width. If the length of the box is 1.35 meters, its height 0.385 meter and its width 0.475 meter, what is the volume of this box?

DIVIDING DECIMAL FRACTIONS

Two decimal fractions can be divided the same way as whole numbers by first making the divisor a whole number by multiplying by a power of ten. Next, multiply the dividend by the same power of ten.

Example 1.   Divide .36 by .12

Solution: $\dfrac{.36}{.12} \times \dfrac{100}{100} = \dfrac{36}{12} = 3$

Example 2.   Divide 12.6 by .063

Solution: $\dfrac{12.6}{.063} \times \dfrac{1000}{1000} = \dfrac{12600}{63} = 200$

Example 3.   Divide .49 by 7

Solution:

$$\begin{array}{r} 0.07 \\ 7\overline{\smash{)}\,.49} \\ \underline{-0} \\ 49 \\ \underline{49} \end{array}$$

When dividing a decimal fraction by a whole
number, the decimal point in the quotient is
placed directly above the decimal point in the
dividend.

DIVIDING DECIMAL FRACTIONS BY POWERS OF TEN

To divide a decimal fraction by 10, 100, 1000
and so on, move the decimal point in the decimal
fraction to the left as many places as there are zeros
in the divisor.

Example 1. $\dfrac{.7}{10} = .07$ $\dfrac{.7}{100} = .007$

Example 2. $\dfrac{3.14}{10} = .314$ $\dfrac{212.4}{1000} = .2124$

50

Perform each of the following.

1. $12.5 \div .125$	2. $49.49 \div 70.7$
3. $2.43 \div .29$	4. $24 \div .006$
5. $11.2 \div .56$	6. $41.2 \div .412$
7. $.126 \div 6$	8. $.17 \div 100$
9. $.42 \div .6$	10. $.05 \div 10$
11. $2.5 \div 25$	12. $25 \div 2.5$

EVALUATING NUMERICAL EXPRESSIONS
(Order of Operations)

Brackets [ ] and parentheses ( ) are sometimes used for grouping numbers. Whatever is enclosed by these symbols should be considered a single quantity.

RULES:

1. Perform grouped operations first, starting with the innermost pair.

2. If there are no groupings, perform operation in the following order. Going from left to right, perform the exponent; then the multiplication or division and then the addition or subtraction.

Examples:

1. 10 - 2 x (9 - 5) = 10 - 2 x 4 = 10 - 8 = 2
   [First subtract 5 from 9]

2. 12 ÷ 3 x 5 = 4 x 5 = 20
   [Working from left to right, divide 12 by 3
   and multiply by 5]

3. 24 - [(17 - 8) + 6] = 24 - [9 + 6] = 24 - 15 = 9
   [First subtract 8 from 17. Add 6 to your
   answer and then subtract from 24]

4. 8 + 10 - (4 + 5) = 8 + 10 - 9 = 18 - 9 = 9

CHAPTER 5
INTRODUCTION TO ALGEBRA

The Fundamental Law of Algebra: basic valid statements used in performing basic operations with numbers.

Commutative Law for Addition states that the sum of two numbers is the same, regardless of the order in which they are added.
$$a + b = b + a$$

Commutative Law for Multiplication states that the product of two numbers is the same, regardless of the order in which they are multiplied.
$$ab = ba$$

Associative Law for Addition states that the sum of three or more numbers is the same, regardless of how they are grouped for additon.
$$a + (b + c) = (a + b) + c$$

Associative Law for Multiplication states that the product of three or more numbers is the same, regardless of how they are grouped for multiplication.
$$a(bc) = (ab)c$$

<u>Distributive Law</u> states that the product of one number and the sum of two or more numbers is equal to the sum of the products of that one number and each of the other numbers.

$$a(b + c) = ab + ac$$
$$r(s + t + u) = rs + rt + ru$$

SYMBOLS/OPERATIONAL SIGNS

< (less than)   > (greater than)
= (equal to)   ≤ (less than and equal to)

$$\frac{+}{+} = +$$ $$\frac{-}{-} = +$$

$$\frac{+}{-} = -$$ $$\frac{-}{+} = -$$

$$+ . + = +$$ $$+ . - = -$$

$$- . - = +$$ $$- . + = -$$

EQUATIONS

An equation is an algebraic statement that one algebraic expression is equal to another.

*To solve an equation, one needs to determine the values of the unknown which satisfy the equation. A value that makes the equation true is called a SOLUTION. The set of values that satisfy the equation is called its SOLUTION SET.

The basic rule is to perform the same operation on both sides of the equation. This means that one can add and subtract the same number on both sides or multiply and divide (non-zero) both sides by the same number.

Example 1. Solve the equation $3x - 4 = x + 8$

Solution:

$$3x - 4 = x + 8$$

$\underline{-x \qquad - x}$ Subtract x from both sides

$$2x - 4 = 8$$

$\underline{+ 4 + 4}$ Add 4 to both sides

$\dfrac{2x}{2} = \dfrac{12}{2}$ Divide both sides by 2

$$x = 6 \ (\text{Ans.})$$

Checking in the original equation, one gets:

$$3(6) - 4 = 6 + 8$$
$$18 - 4 = 14$$
$$14 = 14$$

EXAMPLE 2. Solve the equation $8p - 13 = 3$

Solution:

$$8p - 13 = 3$$

$\underline{+ 13 + 13}$ Add 13 to both sides

$\dfrac{8p}{8} = \dfrac{16}{8}$ Divide both sides by 8

$$p = 2 \ (\text{Ans.})$$

EXAMPLE 3.

Solve the equation $8x - 5 = 2x - (7x - 9)$

Solution:

$8x - 5 = 2x - 7x + 9$ (Remove the parentheses)

$8x - 5 = -5x + 9$

$\underline{5x \qquad + 5x}$ Add 5x to both sides

$13x - 5 = 9$

$\underline{+5 \quad +5}$ Add 5 to both sides

$\dfrac{13x}{13} = \dfrac{14}{13}$ Divide both sides by 13

$$x = \frac{14}{13} \text{ (Ans.)}$$

Solve each equation and check:

1. $x + 5 = 4$

2. $x - 4 = 2$

3. $6x = 18$

4. $3x + 7 = x$

5. $n - 9 = 0$

6. $x - 3 = -6$

7. $\dfrac{t}{3} = 5$

8. $5 - 2t = 3$

9. $\dfrac{1}{2}x = 9$

10. $30 = -6y$

11. $\dfrac{3}{4}x = 3$

12. $-2 = x + 9$

13. $x - 5(x - 3) = 7$

14. $3y = \dfrac{3}{5}$

15. $\dfrac{x}{3} = 10$

16. $2.2y = 66$

17. $-x = 8$

18. $5x - 2 = 13$

19. $6 - 3s = 9$

20. $2(y + 4) = 11$

21. $m + 6 = 6$

22. $m + 6 = -6$

23. $-x = 0$

24. $24y = 12$

CHAPTER 6
INEQUALITIES

The expression a > b is read "a greater than b," and the expression a < b is read "a less than b."

If a and b are real numbers, and a - b is positive, we say a > b. But if a - b is negative, we say a < b.

Two inequalities are said to have the same sense if the signs of inequality point in the same direction.

Example 1.

x + 2 > 4 and x = 1 > 0 have the same sense.

Two inequalities are said to have opposite sense if the signs of inequality point in the opposite directions.

Example 2.

3x - 1 < 2 and x + 1 > 2 have opposite sense.

*The SOLUTION of an inequality are the values of the variable that satisfy the inequality.

Example 3.

The inequality x + 2 > 0 is satisfied by the values
of x greater than -2, written as x > -2

THE NUMBER LINE

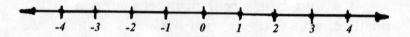

*The numbers associated with the points to the
right of 0 (zero) are the positive integers.

*The numbers associated with the points to the
left of 0 (zero) are the negative integers.

In working with an inequality, we can use tech-
niques similar to those used for solving equations, such as adding the same real number to
both sides or subtracting the same real number
from both sides. We can also multiply both
sides of an inequality by the same positive real
number. Note that multiplication by a negative
number will reverse the sign of the inequality.

Example 4. Solve the inequality x + 3 > 0

Solution: x + 3 > 0
             x + 3 - 3 > 0 - 3   Subtract 3 from
                                      both sides.

                          x > -3 (Ans.)

CHECK: From the number line, we can see that values of x greater than -3 will be located to the right of -3. One of such numbers is -2.

Substituting in the original expression gives:
$$-2 + 3 > 0$$
$$1 > 0 \text{ (true)}$$

Example 5. Solve the inequality $6x - 4 < 8 - x$

Solution: $6x - 4 < 8 - x$
$6x - 4 + 4 < 8 + 4 - x$ Add 4 to both sides
$6x + x < 12 - x + x$ Add x to both sides
$7x < 12$
$\dfrac{7x}{7} < \dfrac{12}{7}$ Divide both sides by 7

$$x < \frac{12}{7} \text{ (Ans.)}$$

Solution consists of all real numbers $x < \dfrac{12}{7}$

Like equations, inequalities can be solved by algebraic and graphical means. The graph of a set of real numbers will represent the points on a number line which correspond to the numbers.

Example 6. Solve the inequality 3x - 2 > 4 and sketch the graph corresponding to the solution.

Solution: 3x - 2 > 4
            3x - 2 + 2 > 4 + 2 Add 2 to both sides
            3x > 6
            $\frac{3x}{3}$ > $\frac{6}{3}$ Divide both sides by 3.

x > 2 (Ans.)

The graph consists of all points to the right of point 2. The parenthesis at point 2 indicates that the point corresponding to 2 is not part of the graph.

*Note that if the solution had included point 2, a bracket [would have been used.

Example 7. Solve the inequality 3x - 7 ≤ x + 1

Solution:
   3x - 7 + 7 ≤ x + 1 + 7   Add 7 to both sides.
   3x ≤ x + 8
   3x - x ≤ x - x + 8   Subtract x from both sides
   2x ≤ 8
   $\frac{2x}{2}$ ≤ $\frac{8}{2}$ divide both sides by 2.

x ≤ 4 (Ans.)

Example 8. Solve the inequality $-6 < 2x - 4 < 2$ and sketch the graph.

Solution:
$$-6 + 4 < 2x - 4 + 4 < 2 + 4 \quad \text{add 4 to each side}$$
$$-2 < 2x < 6$$
$$-2 < 2x < 6 \quad \text{divide each side by 2}$$

$$-1 < x < 3 \text{ (Ans.)}$$

*Solutions are all numbers in the interval (-1,3)

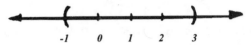

Example 9. Solve the inequality $-3 \leq \dfrac{4 - 3x}{2} < 1$

and sketch the corresponding graph.

Solution:

$$-3 \leq \frac{4 - 3x}{2} < 1$$

$$-3(2) \leq \frac{4 - 3x \ (2)}{2} < 1(2) \quad \text{multiply each side by 2}$$

$$-6 \leq 4 - 3x < 2$$
$$-6 - 4 \leq 4 - 3x - 4 < 2 - 4 \quad \text{subtract 4 from each side}$$
$$-10 \leq -3x < -2$$

$$\frac{-10}{-3} \leq \frac{-3x}{-3} < \frac{-2}{-3}$$

$$\frac{10}{3} \geq x > \frac{2}{3}$$ (note reversed signs)

or

$$\frac{2}{3} < x \leq \frac{10}{3}$$

Example 10. Solve the inequality $\dfrac{x - 3}{x + 4} \geq 0$

Solution: First we can consider the greater than part and then the equality part.

The values of x that satisfy the greater than part are $x > 3$ or $x < -4$ which make the fraction greater than zero.

The value of x that satisfies the equality part is $x = 3$ which makes the fraction equal to zero.

The inequality is therefore satisfied for $x < -4$ or $x \geq 3$.

Solve the following inequalities.

1. $2x - 8 < 0$ 2. $3x + 2 < 4x - 3$

3. $4 - 6x < 16$ 4. $5x - 1 > 2x$

5. $8 - x < x$ 6. $4x > 2$

Solve the following inequalities and sketch the graphs.

7. $4x < 6x - 2$ 8. $\dfrac{x + 5}{x - 1} > 0$

9. $3 > \dfrac{7 - x}{2} \geq 1$ 10. $4x - 3 < 2x + 5$

CHAPTER 7
GRAPHING LINEAR EQUATIONS

THE NUMBER LINE:

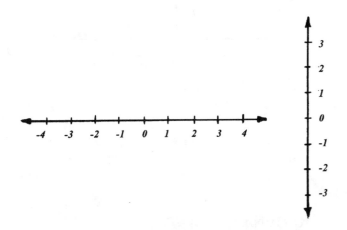

On a horizontal number line, it is customary to use the right side of zero for positive numbers and the left side for negative numbers. On a vertical number line, it is customary to place positive numbers above zero and negative numbers below zero.

THE RECTANGULAR COORDINATE SYSTEM

A rectangular coordinate system is formed by two number lines drawn perpendicular to each other at their zero points, usually referred to as the ORIGIN. The horizontal number line is called the x-axis and the vertical number line is called the y-axis.

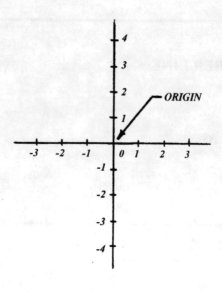

THE COORDINATE PLANE

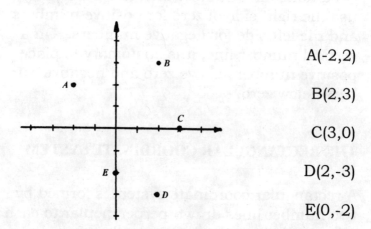

A(-2,2)

B(2,3)

C(3,0)

D(2,-3)

E(0,-2)

Each point in the coordinate plane is associated with an ordered pair of real numbers (x,y). The point B in the above figure is represented by the ordered pair of numbers (2,3). The coordinates of point B are 2 and 3. The first number of the ordered pair, 2, is the x-COORDINATE or the ABSCISSA and the second number of the pair, 3, is the y-COORDINATE or the ORDINATE.

*The coordinates of the origin are (0,0)

*If a point is located on the x-axis, its y-coordinate is 0

*If a point is located on the y-axis, its x-coordinate is 0

Example 1.

Plot the following points on a coordinate system

A (1,5)   B (2,2)   C (3,0)   D (-3,-4)

E (0,6)   F (7,3)   G (-3,1)   H (-2,-1)

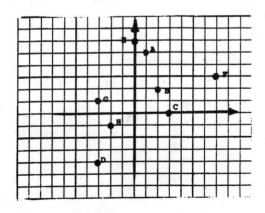

1. Write the coordinates in the form (x,y) for the points shown on the coordinate plane below.

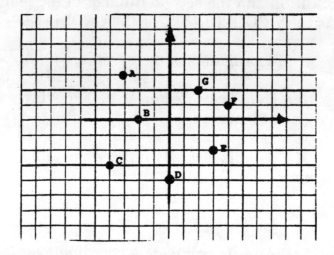

2. If a point is on the x-axis and its abscissa is 6, what is its ordinate?

3. If a point is on the y-axis and its ordinate is -8, what is its abscissa?

4. What are the coordinates of a point located three units to the right of the y-axis and three units below the x-axis?

5. **Plot the following points on a coordinate plane**

A (0,4)   B (3,2)   C (4,4)

D (-1,5)   E (-3,0)   F (-2,-2)

G (-4,-4)   H (0,-3)   I (5,-2)

J (6,-5)

GRAPHS OF LINEAR EQUATIONS

The graph of the equation $y = mx + b$ is a straight line having slope m and y-intercept b. It consists of all points associated with ordered pairs of real numbers.

Example 1. Graph the equation $y = x - 3$

Solution: We will assign values to x and obtain corresponding values for y as shown in the table below. We will plot the ordered pairs and join the points to get a line.

x	y
-3	-6
-2	-5
-1	-4
0	-3
1	-2
2	-1
3	0

-3-3 = -6
-2-3 = -5
-1-3 = -4
0-3 = -3
1-3 = -2
2-3 = -1
3-3 = 0

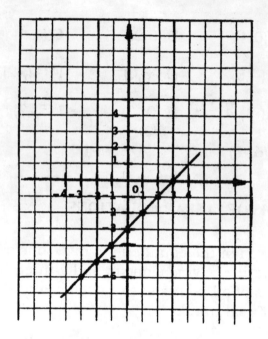

Example 2. Graph y = 5 - x

Solution: Assign values to x to obtain corresponding values for y as shown in table below
and plot the points.

x	y
-2	7
-1	6
0	5
1	4
2	3

$$5 - (-2) = 7$$
$$5 - (-1) = 6$$
$$5 - 0 = 5$$
$$5 - 1 = 4$$
$$5 - 2 = 3$$

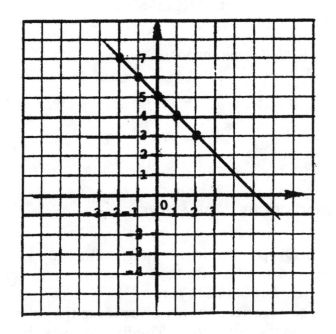

Graph the following equations.

1. $y = x + 2$ 2. $y = x$ 3. $y = 3$

4. $y = 1 + \dfrac{x}{2}$ 5. $y = 5 + x$

THE INTERCEPTS OF A LINE

The graph of a linear equation $ax + by + c = 0$ is a line, where a, b and c are real numbers and a and b are not equal to zero.
*The points where the graph crosses the axes are called its intercepts. The line crosses the x-axis at (a,0) and crosses the y-axis at (0,b).

Example 1. Find the x-intercept and the y-intercept of the line whose equation is $2x - 3y = 6$. Graph the equation to check the answers.

Solution:

STEP 1. To find the x-intercept, set $y = 0$ in the equation.

$$2x - 3y = 6$$
$$2x - 3(0) = 6$$
$$2x = 6$$
$$x = 3$$

The x-intercept is 3.

STEP 2. To find the y-intercept, set x = 0 in the
equation.

$$2x - 3y = 6$$
$$2(0) - 3y = 6$$
$$-3y = 6$$
$$y = -2$$

The y-intercept is -2.

To graph the equation we will assign values to x
to obtain corresponding values for y.

x	y
-3	-4
-2	-3.33
-1	-2.67
0	-2
1	-1.33
2	-0.67
3	0

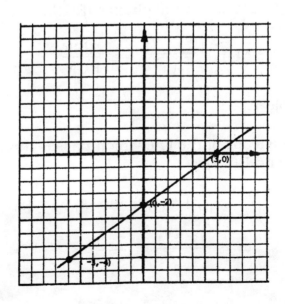

Find the x-intercept and the y-intercept for each of the following.

1. $2x - 3y - 4 = 0$ 2. $3y = -x + 2$

3. $3x - 2y = 4$ 4. $2x - 5y = 8$

THE SLOPE OF A LINE

The SLOPE of a line measures the steepness of the line and is defined as the vertical directed distance from one point to another on a straight line divided by the horizontal directed distance from the first point to the second point. Simply stated, SLOPE is the ratio of the vertical change (RISE) to the horizontal change (RUN).

$$m = \frac{y_2 - y_1}{x_2 - x_1} = \frac{RISE}{RUN}$$

Example 1.

Find the slope of the line which passes through A(6,9) and B(5,7).

Solution: Let $(x_1, y_1) = (6,9)$ and $(x_2, y_2) = (5,7)$

SLOPE, $m = \dfrac{y_2 - y_1}{x_2 - x_1} = \dfrac{7 - 9}{5 - 6} = \dfrac{-2}{-1} = 2$

76

Example 2.

Find the slope of the line which passes through A(-5,-2) and B(6,4). Plot points A and B

Solution: Let $(x_1,y_1) = (-5,-2)$ and $(x_2,y_2) = (6,4)$

SLOPE, $m = \dfrac{y_2 - y_1}{x_2 - x_1} = \dfrac{4 - (-2)}{6 - (-5)} = \dfrac{4 + 2}{6 + 5} = \dfrac{6}{11}$

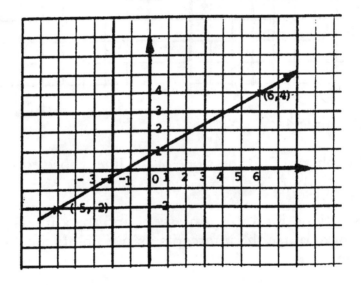

Example 3.

Find the slope of the line whose equation is y = 2.

Solution: Let $(x_1,y_1) = (1,2)$ and $(x_2,y_2) = (-1,2)$

SLOPE, $m = \dfrac{y_2 - y_1}{x_2 - x_1} = \dfrac{2 - 2}{-1 - 1} = \dfrac{0}{-2} = 0$

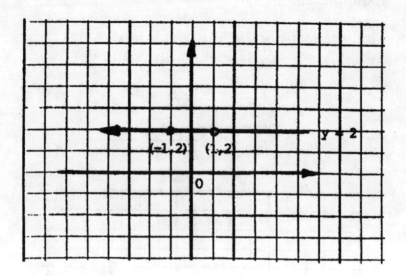

Example 4.

Graph and find the slope of the line whose equation is $3x + 4y = 12$

Solution: Find the y-intercept and the x-intercept and use the intercepts as two points for the line.

For the x-intercept, set $y = 0$ in the equation.
$$3x + 4(0) = 12$$
$$3x = 12$$
$$x = 4$$

The x-intercept is $(4,0)$

For the y-intercept, set x = 0 in the equation.

$$3(0) + 4y = 12$$
$$4y = 12$$
$$y = 3$$

The y-intercept is (0,3)

Let $(x_1, y_1) = (0,3)$ and $(x_2, y_2) = (4,0)$

SLOPE, $m = \dfrac{y_2 - y_1}{x_2 - x_1} = \dfrac{0 - 3}{4 - 0} = \dfrac{-3}{4}$ (negative slope)

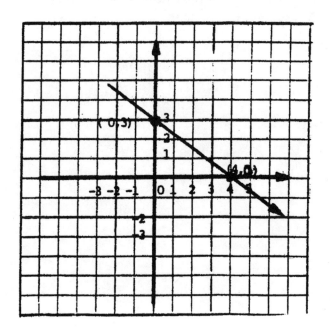

Plot points A and B in each of the following and find the slope of the line passing through the points.

1. A(O,-3) B(5,3)   2. A(-3,8) B(-2,7)

3. A(3,2) B(4,-5)   4. A(-1,-4) B(-4,-1)

5. Find the slope of the line whose equation is
   $2x - 3y - 6 = 0$

ANSWERS TO PROBLEMS

EXERCISES 1-1 (Page 5)

1. 1,000,000 mm
2. 0.7 cm
3. 1 m
4. 0.675 l
5. 0.86 l
6. 5.0 l
7. 1,000,000 mg
8. 1,400 g
9. 500 g
10. 1.0 km
11. 10 oz.
12. 20 qt.
13. 15,840 ft.
14. 10 pt.
15. 440 yd.
16. 6.7 km
17. 81.28 mm
18. 31.17 sq. ft.
19. 0.264 gal.
20. 0.45 kg

EXERCISES 1-2 (Page 13)

1. 33.6 cm
2. 33.2 m

3. 441.3 yd
4. 45.84 cm
5. 26.4 in.
6. 22.4 cm
7. 9.27 sq. cm
8. 66 sq. m
9. 10.5 sq. in.
10. 6.48 sq. ft.
11. 1962.5 sq. mm
12. 45.3 sq. in.
13. 150.72 cu. cm
14. 14.4 cu. ft.

EXERCISES 2-1 (Page 31)

1. 75°
2. 11°
3. 40°
4. 43°
5. 109°
6. 45°
7. 95°
8. 125°
9. (a) 32°
   (b) 148°
   (c) 32°
   (d) 148°

EXERCISES 3-1 (Page 36)

1. Simple
2. Simple
3. Simple
4. Complex
5. Complex
6. Complex
7. Complex
8. $\dfrac{15}{21}$
9. $\dfrac{42}{50}$
10. $\dfrac{28}{12}$
11. $\dfrac{25}{75}$
12. $\dfrac{33}{99}$
13. $\dfrac{12}{30}$
14. $\dfrac{4}{3}$
15. $\dfrac{20}{31}$
16. $\dfrac{4}{7}$
17. $\dfrac{5}{9}$
18. $\dfrac{1}{5}$
19. $\dfrac{40}{81}$
20. $\dfrac{9}{7}$
21. Yes
22. Yes
23. No
24. Yes

EXERCISES 3-2 (Page 40)

1. $\dfrac{7}{6}$
2. $\dfrac{11}{8}$
3. $\dfrac{13}{10}$
4. $1\dfrac{5}{7}$
5. $5\dfrac{1}{18}$
6. $5\dfrac{3}{4}$
7. 3
8. $1\dfrac{7}{12}$

EXERCISES 3-3 (Page 42)

1. $\dfrac{5}{8}$

2. $\dfrac{2}{7}$

3. $1\dfrac{1}{5}$

4. $3\dfrac{7}{8}$

5. $7\dfrac{3}{16}$

6. $1\dfrac{2}{3}$

EXERCISES 3-4 (Page 44)

1. $2\dfrac{2}{5}$

2. $12\dfrac{1}{4}$

3. $1\dfrac{41}{45}$

4. 1

5. $\dfrac{3}{10}$

6. $\dfrac{13}{15}$

7. 2 qts.

EXERCISES 4-1 (Page 49)

1. 0.034
2. 16.14
3. 0.3
4. 0.0003
5. 0.0288
6. 314
7. 0.247 cu. m

EXERCISES 4-2 (Page 51)

1. 100
2. 0.7
3. 8.38
4. 4000
5. 20
6. 100
7. 0.021
8. 0.0017
9. 0.70
10. 0.005
11. 0.1
12. 10

EXERCISES 5-1 (Page 57)

1. -1
2. 6

3. 3
4. -3.5
5. 9
6. -3
7. 15
8. 1
9. 18
10. –5
11. 4
12. -11
13. 2
14. $\dfrac{1}{5}$
15. 30
16. 30
17. –8
18. 3
19. –1
20. 1.5
21. 0
22. –12
23. 0
24. 0.5

EXERCISES 6-1 (Page 65)

1. x < 4
2. x > 5
3. x ≥ 2
4. x > $\dfrac{1}{3}$
5. x > 4

6. x > $\dfrac{1}{2}$
7. x > 1
8. x < -5, x > 1
9. 1 < x ≤ 5
10. x < 4

EXERCISES 7-1 (Page 70)

1. A(-3,3),
   B(-2,0),
   C(-4,-3),
   D(0, -4),
   E(3,-2),
   F(4,1),
   G(2,2)
2. 0
3. 0
4. (3, -3)

5.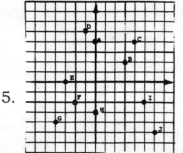

EXERCISES 7-2 (Page 74)

1.

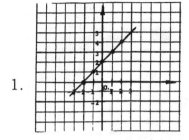

5.

2.

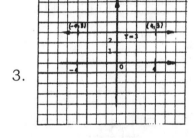

3.

4.

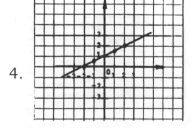

EXERCISES 7-3 (Page 76)

1. x-intercept is   2
   y-intercept is - $\frac{3}{4}$

2. x-intercept is   2
   y-intercept is $\frac{2}{3}$

3. x-intercept is $\frac{4}{3}$
   y-intercept is -2

4. x-intercept is   4
   y-intercept is - $\frac{8}{5}$

EXERCISES 7-4 (Page 80)

3. slope = -7

1. slope = $\frac{6}{5}$

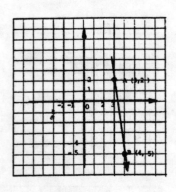

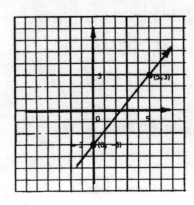

4. slope = -1

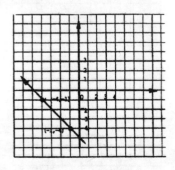

2. slope = -1

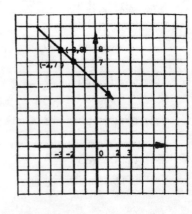

5. slope = 2/3

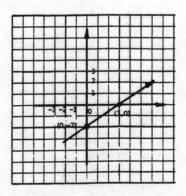

INDEX

Abscissa 69
Addition of Fractions 37
Adjacent Angles 28
Algebraic Expression 54
Alternate Interior Angles 25
Angle 21
    acute 22
    obtuse 23
    right 22
    straight 23
Area 3, 6
    of circle 7
    of parallelogram 7
    of rectangle 6
    of square 8
    of triangle 6
Associative Law 53
Circle 7, 12
    area of 7
Circumference 12
Commutative Law 53
Complementary Angles 25
Coordinate Plane 68, 69
Corresponding Angles 25
Cylinder 8, 10
Decimal Fractions 47
    division of 49
    multiplication of 48
Distributive Law 54
Equations 54

Equivalent Fraction 38
Fractions 33
    addition of 37
    division of 45
    improper 34
    multiplication of 42
    proper 34
    simple 34
    subtraction of 40
Fundamental Law of Algebra 53
Inequalities 59
Intercept of a Line 74
Lines 19
    intersecting 19, 24
    parallel 19, 20
    skew 19, 20
Measures 1-3
    customary units 1-3
    metric units 1-3
Number Line 60, 67
Ordinate 69
Parallelogram 7
    area of 7
Perimeters 11
    of polygon 11
Prism 9
Rectangle 6
    area of 6
Rectangular Coordinate 67
Right Angle 22
Slope of a Line 76
Supplementary Angles 27
Triangle 6
    area of 6
Vertical Angles 30

Volume 9
    of cone 9
    of cylinder 10
    of prism 9, 10
    of sphere 10
x-intercept 74, 76
y-intercept 74, 76

ABOUT THE AUTHOR

Ted A. Akinyanju is a professor
in the Department of Technology
at Norfolk State University.

He is a member of professional
and honor societies.